50 Pasta Dishes for Every Mood

By: Kelly Johnson

Table of Contents

- Spaghetti Aglio e Olio
- Creamy Alfredo Pasta
- Spaghetti Bolognese
- Pesto Penne
- Mac and Cheese
- Fettuccine Carbonara
- Lasagna
- Pasta Primavera
- Shrimp Scampi
- Caprese Pasta Salad
- Penne Arrabbiata
- Spaghetti and Meatballs
- Lobster Ravioli
- Gnocchi with Brown Butter Sage Sauce
- Spinach and Ricotta Stuffed Shells
- Fettuccine with Roasted Red Pepper Sauce
- Ziti with Sausage and Peppers
- Chicken Parmesan
- Pappardelle with Mushroom Sauce
- Cajun Chicken Pasta
- Shrimp and Asparagus Linguine
- Baked Ziti
- Penne alla Vodka
- Fettuccine Alfredo with Broccoli
- Butternut Squash Ravioli with Sage Butter
- Spinach and Artichoke Pasta
- Pasta with Puttanesca Sauce
- Cacio e Pepe
- Macaroni and Beef
- Pasta Primavera with Lemon and Garlic
- Spaghetti Puttanesca
- Tortellini in Brodo
- Baked Manicotti
- Pasta with Clams
- Spaghetti with Anchovies and Garlic

- Eggplant Parmesan Pasta
- Seafood Pasta
- Ricotta and Spinach Cannelloni
- Pasta with Sun-Dried Tomato Pesto
- Pesto Lasagna
- Fusilli with Sausage and Broccoli Rabe
- Gnocchi with Tomato Basil Sauce
- Tortellini with Pesto and Peas
- Pasta Carbonara with Peas
- Spaghetti alla Caprese
- Roasted Garlic Pasta with Mushrooms
- Pesto Mac and Cheese
- Pasta with Spicy Sausage and Kale
- Spaghetti with Lemon and Parmesan
- Vegan Alfredo Pasta

Spaghetti Aglio e Olio

Ingredients:

- 8 oz spaghetti
- 1/4 cup olive oil
- 6 garlic cloves, thinly sliced
- 1/4 teaspoon red pepper flakes
- Salt and pepper to taste
- 1/4 cup fresh parsley, chopped
- Freshly grated Parmesan cheese (optional)

Instructions:

1. Cook spaghetti according to package instructions. Drain, reserving some pasta water.
2. In a large pan, heat olive oil over medium heat. Add garlic and sauté until golden brown.
3. Add red pepper flakes, salt, and pepper. Toss in the cooked spaghetti, adding reserved pasta water as needed.
4. Stir in fresh parsley and top with Parmesan cheese if desired. Serve immediately.

Creamy Alfredo Pasta

Ingredients:

- 8 oz fettuccine
- 2 tablespoons butter
- 1 cup heavy cream
- 1 cup grated Parmesan cheese
- 1 teaspoon garlic powder
- Salt and pepper to taste
- Fresh parsley, chopped (optional)

Instructions:

1. Cook fettuccine according to package instructions. Drain.
2. In a pan, melt butter over medium heat. Add heavy cream and bring to a simmer.
3. Stir in Parmesan cheese, garlic powder, salt, and pepper. Cook until the sauce thickens.
4. Toss pasta with sauce, top with parsley if desired, and serve.

Spaghetti Bolognese

Ingredients:

- 1 lb ground beef or pork
- 1 onion, chopped
- 2 garlic cloves, minced
- 1 carrot, chopped
- 1 celery stalk, chopped
- 1 can (14.5 oz) crushed tomatoes
- 1/2 cup red wine (optional)
- 1 teaspoon Italian seasoning
- Salt and pepper to taste
- 8 oz spaghetti

Instructions:

1. Cook spaghetti according to package instructions. Drain.
2. In a large pan, cook ground meat over medium heat until browned. Add onion, garlic, carrot, and celery, and sauté until soft.
3. Add crushed tomatoes, red wine, Italian seasoning, salt, and pepper. Simmer for 30 minutes, stirring occasionally.
4. Serve the sauce over cooked spaghetti.

Pesto Penne

Ingredients:

- 8 oz penne pasta
- 1/2 cup pesto sauce
- 1/4 cup grated Parmesan cheese
- 1 tablespoon olive oil
- Pine nuts for garnish (optional)

Instructions:

1. Cook penne pasta according to package instructions. Drain.
2. Toss pasta with pesto sauce, Parmesan cheese, and olive oil.
3. Garnish with pine nuts if desired and serve immediately.

Mac and Cheese

Ingredients:

- 8 oz elbow macaroni
- 2 tablespoons butter
- 2 tablespoons all-purpose flour
- 2 cups milk
- 2 cups shredded cheddar cheese
- Salt and pepper to taste

Instructions:

1. Cook macaroni according to package instructions. Drain.
2. In a pan, melt butter over medium heat. Whisk in flour and cook for 1-2 minutes.
3. Gradually add milk, whisking constantly, until the mixture thickens.
4. Stir in cheddar cheese, salt, and pepper. Toss with macaroni and serve.

Fettuccine Carbonara

Ingredients:

- 8 oz fettuccine
- 4 oz pancetta or bacon, diced
- 2 eggs
- 1/2 cup grated Parmesan cheese
- 1/4 teaspoon black pepper
- Salt to taste
- Fresh parsley, chopped (optional)

Instructions:

1. Cook fettuccine according to package instructions. Drain, reserving some pasta water.
2. In a pan, cook pancetta or bacon until crispy. Remove from heat.
3. Whisk eggs, Parmesan, pepper, and salt in a bowl.
4. Toss the pasta with the egg mixture, adding reserved pasta water as needed. Stir in pancetta.
5. Serve with parsley if desired.

Lasagna

Ingredients:

- 12 lasagna noodles
- 1 lb ground beef
- 1 onion, chopped
- 1 can (14.5 oz) crushed tomatoes
- 1 can (6 oz) tomato paste
- 1 teaspoon garlic powder
- 2 teaspoons Italian seasoning
- 1 cup ricotta cheese
- 2 cups shredded mozzarella cheese
- 1/2 cup grated Parmesan cheese
- Salt and pepper to taste

Instructions:

1. Preheat oven to 375°F (190°C). Cook lasagna noodles according to package instructions. Drain.
2. In a pan, cook ground beef and onion over medium heat until browned. Stir in crushed tomatoes, tomato paste, garlic powder, Italian seasoning, salt, and pepper. Simmer for 20 minutes.
3. In a baking dish, layer noodles, meat sauce, ricotta cheese, mozzarella cheese, and Parmesan cheese.
4. Repeat layers and top with mozzarella and Parmesan. Bake for 30 minutes. Let cool before serving.

Pasta Primavera

Ingredients:

- 8 oz pasta (penne, spaghetti, or fusilli)
- 1 tablespoon olive oil
- 1 zucchini, sliced
- 1 red bell pepper, sliced
- 1 cup cherry tomatoes, halved
- 1/2 cup Parmesan cheese
- Salt and pepper to taste
- Fresh basil, chopped (optional)

Instructions:

1. Cook pasta according to package instructions. Drain.
2. Heat olive oil in a pan and sauté zucchini, bell pepper, and cherry tomatoes until tender.
3. Toss cooked pasta with vegetables, Parmesan, salt, and pepper.
4. Garnish with fresh basil if desired and serve.

Shrimp Scampi

Ingredients:

- 8 oz spaghetti
- 1 lb shrimp, peeled and deveined
- 4 tablespoons butter
- 4 garlic cloves, minced
- 1/4 teaspoon red pepper flakes
- 1/4 cup white wine
- 1/4 cup fresh parsley, chopped
- Salt and pepper to taste

Instructions:

1. Cook spaghetti according to package instructions. Drain.
2. In a pan, melt butter over medium heat. Add garlic and red pepper flakes, and sauté for 1 minute.
3. Add shrimp and cook until pink, about 3-4 minutes.
4. Pour in white wine and cook for 1-2 minutes. Toss cooked pasta with shrimp and sauce.
5. Garnish with parsley and serve.

Caprese Pasta Salad

Ingredients:

- 8 oz pasta (penne, fusilli, or farfalle)
- 1 cup cherry tomatoes, halved
- 1/2 cup fresh mozzarella, cubed
- 1/4 cup fresh basil, chopped
- 1/4 cup balsamic vinegar
- 2 tablespoons olive oil
- Salt and pepper to taste

Instructions:

1. Cook pasta according to package instructions. Drain and let cool.
2. Toss pasta with cherry tomatoes, mozzarella, basil, balsamic vinegar, olive oil, salt, and pepper.
3. Chill for 30 minutes before serving.

Penne Arrabbiata

Ingredients:

- 8 oz penne pasta
- 2 tablespoons olive oil
- 4 garlic cloves, minced
- 1 can (14.5 oz) crushed tomatoes
- 1/2 teaspoon red pepper flakes
- 1/4 cup fresh parsley, chopped
- Salt to taste

Instructions:

1. Cook penne pasta according to package instructions. Drain.
2. In a pan, heat olive oil over medium heat and sauté garlic until golden.
3. Add crushed tomatoes and red pepper flakes. Simmer for 15 minutes.
4. Toss pasta with sauce, parsley, and salt. Serve immediately.

Spaghetti and Meatballs

Ingredients:

- 8 oz spaghetti
- 1 lb ground beef or pork
- 1/4 cup breadcrumbs
- 1/4 cup grated Parmesan cheese
- 1 egg
- 2 garlic cloves, minced
- 1 can (14.5 oz) crushed tomatoes
- 1 teaspoon Italian seasoning
- Salt and pepper to taste
- 1 tablespoon olive oil

Instructions:

1. Preheat the oven to 375°F (190°C). In a bowl, mix ground meat, breadcrumbs, Parmesan cheese, egg, garlic, salt, and pepper. Form into meatballs.
2. Place meatballs on a baking sheet and bake for 20 minutes, until golden brown.
3. While meatballs bake, heat olive oil in a pan over medium heat. Add crushed tomatoes, Italian seasoning, salt, and pepper. Simmer for 15 minutes.
4. Add baked meatballs to the sauce and cook for 5-10 minutes.
5. Serve meatballs and sauce over cooked spaghetti.

Lobster Ravioli

Ingredients:

- 1 package lobster ravioli
- 2 tablespoons butter
- 1/2 cup heavy cream
- 1/4 cup Parmesan cheese
- 1 teaspoon lemon zest
- Salt and pepper to taste

Instructions:

1. Cook lobster ravioli according to package instructions. Drain.
2. In a pan, melt butter over medium heat. Stir in heavy cream and cook for 2-3 minutes.
3. Add Parmesan cheese, lemon zest, salt, and pepper. Stir until cheese melts and sauce thickens.
4. Toss cooked ravioli in the sauce and serve immediately.

Gnocchi with Brown Butter Sage Sauce

Ingredients:

- 1 package gnocchi
- 1/4 cup butter
- 10 fresh sage leaves
- 1/4 cup grated Parmesan cheese
- Salt and pepper to taste

Instructions:

1. Cook gnocchi according to package instructions. Drain.
2. In a pan, melt butter over medium heat. Add sage leaves and cook until the butter becomes brown and fragrant.
3. Toss gnocchi in the brown butter sauce. Add Parmesan, salt, and pepper.
4. Serve immediately, garnished with extra Parmesan.

Spinach and Ricotta Stuffed Shells

Ingredients:

- 12 jumbo pasta shells
- 1 cup ricotta cheese
- 1 cup cooked spinach, chopped
- 1 egg
- 2 cups marinara sauce
- 1/2 cup shredded mozzarella cheese
- 1/4 cup grated Parmesan cheese
- Salt and pepper to taste

Instructions:

1. Preheat the oven to 375°F (190°C). Cook pasta shells according to package instructions. Drain and set aside.
2. In a bowl, mix ricotta, spinach, egg, salt, and pepper.
3. Stuff each pasta shell with the ricotta mixture and place in a baking dish.
4. Pour marinara sauce over the shells and top with mozzarella and Parmesan cheese.
5. Bake for 20-25 minutes until bubbly and golden.

Fettuccine with Roasted Red Pepper Sauce

Ingredients:

- 8 oz fettuccine
- 2 roasted red peppers, peeled and chopped
- 1/2 cup heavy cream
- 1 tablespoon olive oil
- 2 garlic cloves, minced
- 1/4 cup Parmesan cheese
- Salt and pepper to taste

Instructions:

1. Cook fettuccine according to package instructions. Drain.
2. In a blender, blend roasted red peppers and heavy cream until smooth.
3. In a pan, heat olive oil over medium heat and sauté garlic until fragrant. Add the red pepper sauce, Parmesan, salt, and pepper. Simmer for 5 minutes.
4. Toss cooked fettuccine in the sauce and serve.

Ziti with Sausage and Peppers

Ingredients:

- 8 oz ziti pasta
- 1 lb Italian sausage, casings removed
- 1 red bell pepper, sliced
- 1 yellow bell pepper, sliced
- 1 onion, chopped
- 2 garlic cloves, minced
- 1 can (14.5 oz) crushed tomatoes
- 1/2 teaspoon Italian seasoning
- Salt and pepper to taste
- 1/4 cup grated Parmesan cheese

Instructions:

1. Cook ziti according to package instructions. Drain.
2. In a pan, cook sausage over medium heat until browned. Remove and set aside.
3. In the same pan, sauté bell peppers, onion, and garlic until soft.
4. Add crushed tomatoes, Italian seasoning, salt, and pepper. Simmer for 10 minutes.
5. Stir in cooked sausage and pasta. Serve with grated Parmesan.

Chicken Parmesan

Ingredients:

- 2 chicken breasts, breaded and fried
- 1 cup marinara sauce
- 1/2 cup shredded mozzarella cheese
- 1/4 cup grated Parmesan cheese
- 1 tablespoon olive oil

Instructions:

1. Preheat the oven to 375°F (190°C).
2. Fry breaded chicken breasts in olive oil until golden brown.
3. Place chicken in a baking dish, top with marinara sauce, mozzarella, and Parmesan cheese.
4. Bake for 20 minutes or until cheese is bubbly and golden.
5. Serve with pasta or a side salad.

Pappardelle with Mushroom Sauce

Ingredients:

- 8 oz pappardelle pasta
- 1 lb mushrooms, sliced
- 2 tablespoons butter
- 1/2 cup heavy cream
- 1/4 cup Parmesan cheese
- 2 garlic cloves, minced
- Salt and pepper to taste
- Fresh parsley, chopped (optional)

Instructions:

1. Cook pappardelle according to package instructions. Drain.
2. In a pan, melt butter over medium heat. Sauté garlic and mushrooms until soft.
3. Add heavy cream and cook until sauce thickens. Stir in Parmesan, salt, and pepper.
4. Toss pasta with the sauce and garnish with fresh parsley if desired.

Cajun Chicken Pasta

Ingredients:

- 2 chicken breasts, sliced
- 8 oz fettuccine
- 2 tablespoons Cajun seasoning
- 1 tablespoon olive oil
- 1/2 cup heavy cream
- 1/2 cup Parmesan cheese
- Salt and pepper to taste

Instructions:

1. Cook fettuccine according to package instructions. Drain.
2. Toss chicken in Cajun seasoning. In a pan, heat olive oil over medium heat and cook chicken until browned and cooked through.
3. Remove chicken and add heavy cream to the pan. Stir in Parmesan cheese, salt, and pepper.
4. Toss cooked pasta with the sauce and chicken. Serve immediately.

Shrimp and Asparagus Linguine

Ingredients:

- 8 oz linguine pasta
- 1 lb shrimp, peeled and deveined
- 1 bunch asparagus, chopped
- 2 tablespoons olive oil
- 2 garlic cloves, minced
- 1/2 cup white wine
- 1/4 cup Parmesan cheese
- Salt and pepper to taste

Instructions:

1. Cook linguine according to package instructions. Drain.
2. In a pan, heat olive oil over medium heat. Sauté garlic and asparagus until tender.
3. Add shrimp and cook until pink. Pour in white wine and cook for 2 minutes.
4. Toss cooked pasta with the shrimp mixture and Parmesan cheese. Serve immediately.

Baked Ziti

Ingredients:

- 1 lb ziti pasta
- 2 cups marinara sauce
- 1 lb ricotta cheese
- 1 cup shredded mozzarella cheese
- 1/4 cup grated Parmesan cheese
- 1 tablespoon olive oil
- 1/2 teaspoon Italian seasoning
- 1/4 cup fresh basil, chopped (optional)

Instructions:

1. Preheat the oven to 375°F (190°C). Cook ziti according to package instructions. Drain.
2. In a bowl, mix ricotta cheese, mozzarella, Parmesan, Italian seasoning, and marinara sauce.
3. Toss cooked ziti in the sauce mixture, then transfer to a baking dish.
4. Top with extra mozzarella and Parmesan. Bake for 25-30 minutes, or until golden and bubbly.
5. Garnish with fresh basil and serve.

Penne alla Vodka

Ingredients:

- 8 oz penne pasta
- 1 tablespoon olive oil
- 1/2 onion, chopped
- 2 garlic cloves, minced
- 1/2 cup vodka
- 1 can (14.5 oz) crushed tomatoes
- 1/2 cup heavy cream
- 1/4 cup grated Parmesan cheese
- Salt and pepper to taste

Instructions:

1. Cook penne according to package instructions. Drain.
2. In a pan, heat olive oil over medium heat. Sauté onion and garlic until soft.
3. Add vodka and cook for 2-3 minutes to reduce. Stir in crushed tomatoes and simmer for 10 minutes.
4. Add heavy cream, Parmesan, salt, and pepper. Stir until creamy.
5. Toss pasta in the sauce and serve immediately.

Fettuccine Alfredo with Broccoli

Ingredients:

- 8 oz fettuccine
- 1 cup broccoli florets
- 2 tablespoons butter
- 1 cup heavy cream
- 1/2 cup grated Parmesan cheese
- Salt and pepper to taste

Instructions:

1. Cook fettuccine and broccoli in boiling water according to package instructions. Drain.
2. In a pan, melt butter over medium heat. Add heavy cream and simmer for 2-3 minutes.
3. Stir in Parmesan cheese, salt, and pepper, and cook until sauce thickens.
4. Toss cooked pasta and broccoli in the sauce and serve.

Butternut Squash Ravioli with Sage Butter

Ingredients:

- 1 package butternut squash ravioli
- 1/4 cup butter
- 10 fresh sage leaves
- 1/4 cup Parmesan cheese, grated
- Salt and pepper to taste

Instructions:

1. Cook ravioli according to package instructions. Drain.
2. In a pan, melt butter over medium heat. Add sage leaves and cook until the butter turns golden and fragrant.
3. Toss cooked ravioli in the sage butter, then sprinkle with Parmesan, salt, and pepper.
4. Serve immediately.

Spinach and Artichoke Pasta

Ingredients:

- 8 oz pasta (penne or rigatoni)
- 1 can (14 oz) artichoke hearts, drained and chopped
- 2 cups fresh spinach, chopped
- 2 tablespoons olive oil
- 2 garlic cloves, minced
- 1/2 cup heavy cream
- 1/2 cup grated Parmesan cheese
- Salt and pepper to taste

Instructions:

1. Cook pasta according to package instructions. Drain.
2. In a pan, heat olive oil over medium heat and sauté garlic until fragrant. Add spinach and cook until wilted.
3. Stir in artichokes, heavy cream, Parmesan, salt, and pepper. Simmer for 5 minutes.
4. Toss pasta in the sauce and serve immediately.

Pasta with Puttanesca Sauce

Ingredients:

- 8 oz pasta (spaghetti or penne)
- 1 tablespoon olive oil
- 1/2 onion, chopped
- 2 garlic cloves, minced
- 1 can (14.5 oz) diced tomatoes
- 1/4 cup Kalamata olives, chopped
- 2 tablespoons capers
- 1/4 teaspoon red pepper flakes
- 1 tablespoon fresh parsley, chopped
- Salt and pepper to taste

Instructions:

1. Cook pasta according to package instructions. Drain.
2. In a pan, heat olive oil over medium heat. Sauté onion and garlic until soft.
3. Add diced tomatoes, olives, capers, red pepper flakes, salt, and pepper. Simmer for 10 minutes.
4. Toss pasta with the sauce and garnish with fresh parsley. Serve immediately.

Cacio e Pepe

Ingredients:

- 8 oz spaghetti
- 1/2 cup Pecorino Romano cheese, grated
- 1 tablespoon black pepper
- Salt to taste
- 1 tablespoon butter

Instructions:

1. Cook spaghetti according to package instructions. Reserve 1/2 cup pasta water before draining.
2. In a pan, melt butter and add black pepper. Toast pepper for 1-2 minutes.
3. Add reserved pasta water to the pan, then stir in grated cheese until smooth.
4. Toss cooked spaghetti in the sauce, adding more pasta water if necessary. Serve immediately.

Macaroni and Beef

Ingredients:

- 8 oz elbow macaroni
- 1 lb ground beef
- 1/2 onion, chopped
- 1 can (14.5 oz) diced tomatoes
- 1 tablespoon tomato paste
- 1 teaspoon Italian seasoning
- Salt and pepper to taste

Instructions:

1. Cook macaroni according to package instructions. Drain.
2. In a pan, cook ground beef and onion until browned. Drain excess fat.
3. Stir in diced tomatoes, tomato paste, Italian seasoning, salt, and pepper. Simmer for 10 minutes.
4. Toss cooked macaroni in the beef mixture and serve.

Pasta Primavera with Lemon and Garlic

Ingredients:

- 8 oz pasta (spaghetti or penne)
- 1 tablespoon olive oil
- 1 zucchini, sliced
- 1 red bell pepper, sliced
- 1/2 onion, chopped
- 2 garlic cloves, minced
- 1/2 lemon, juiced
- 1/4 cup fresh parsley, chopped
- Salt and pepper to taste

Instructions:

1. Cook pasta according to package instructions. Drain.
2. In a pan, heat olive oil over medium heat. Sauté zucchini, bell pepper, and onion until tender.
3. Add garlic, lemon juice, salt, and pepper. Cook for 1-2 minutes.
4. Toss cooked pasta with the vegetables and garnish with parsley. Serve immediately.

Spaghetti Puttanesca

Ingredients:

- 8 oz spaghetti
- 1 tablespoon olive oil
- 2 garlic cloves, minced
- 1 can (14.5 oz) crushed tomatoes
- 1/4 cup Kalamata olives, chopped
- 2 tablespoons capers
- 1/4 teaspoon red pepper flakes
- Salt and pepper to taste

Instructions:

1. Cook spaghetti according to package instructions. Drain.
2. In a pan, heat olive oil over medium heat. Sauté garlic until fragrant.
3. Add crushed tomatoes, olives, capers, red pepper flakes, salt, and pepper. Simmer for 10 minutes.
4. Toss pasta with the sauce and serve.

Tortellini in Brodo

Ingredients:

- 1 lb fresh tortellini
- 6 cups chicken broth
- 2 tablespoons olive oil
- 1/2 onion, chopped
- 1 garlic clove, minced
- Fresh parsley, chopped for garnish
- Salt and pepper to taste

Instructions:

1. In a pot, heat olive oil over medium heat. Sauté onion and garlic until soft.
2. Add chicken broth and bring to a boil. Reduce heat and simmer for 10 minutes.
3. Add fresh tortellini and cook according to package instructions (usually 3-4 minutes).
4. Season with salt and pepper to taste. Serve in bowls and garnish with chopped parsley.

Baked Manicotti

Ingredients:

- 12 manicotti shells
- 1 1/2 cups ricotta cheese
- 1 cup shredded mozzarella cheese
- 1/4 cup grated Parmesan cheese
- 1 egg
- 2 cups marinara sauce
- 1 tablespoon fresh basil, chopped
- Salt and pepper to taste

Instructions:

1. Preheat the oven to 375°F (190°C). Cook manicotti shells according to package instructions. Drain and set aside.
2. In a bowl, combine ricotta, mozzarella, Parmesan, egg, basil, salt, and pepper.
3. Stuff cooked manicotti shells with the cheese mixture and place them in a baking dish.
4. Pour marinara sauce over the stuffed shells. Cover with foil and bake for 25 minutes.
5. Remove foil, sprinkle with extra mozzarella cheese, and bake for an additional 10 minutes until bubbly and golden.

Pasta with Clams

Ingredients:

- 8 oz spaghetti or linguine
- 2 tablespoons olive oil
- 4 garlic cloves, minced
- 1/2 cup white wine
- 1 lb fresh clams, scrubbed
- 1/4 cup fresh parsley, chopped
- Red pepper flakes (optional)
- Salt and pepper to taste

Instructions:

1. Cook pasta according to package instructions. Drain, reserving some pasta water.
2. In a large pan, heat olive oil over medium heat. Sauté garlic until fragrant.
3. Add white wine and clams. Cover and cook for 5-7 minutes until clams open.
4. Toss cooked pasta with clams, adding reserved pasta water as needed. Season with salt, pepper, parsley, and red pepper flakes.
5. Serve immediately.

Spaghetti with Anchovies and Garlic

Ingredients:

- 8 oz spaghetti
- 4 tablespoons olive oil
- 4 garlic cloves, sliced
- 6 anchovy fillets
- 1/2 teaspoon red pepper flakes (optional)
- Salt and pepper to taste
- Fresh parsley, chopped for garnish

Instructions:

1. Cook spaghetti according to package instructions. Drain, reserving some pasta water.
2. In a pan, heat olive oil over medium heat. Sauté garlic until fragrant, then add anchovies. Mash anchovies with a spoon until they dissolve into the oil.
3. Add red pepper flakes, salt, and pepper. Toss cooked pasta in the sauce, adding reserved pasta water as needed to coat.
4. Garnish with fresh parsley and serve.

Eggplant Parmesan Pasta

Ingredients:

- 8 oz penne or spaghetti
- 2 medium eggplants, sliced and breaded
- 2 cups marinara sauce
- 1 cup shredded mozzarella cheese
- 1/4 cup grated Parmesan cheese
- 2 tablespoons olive oil
- Salt and pepper to taste

Instructions:

1. Preheat the oven to 375°F (190°C). Bread eggplant slices and bake for 20-25 minutes until crispy.
2. Cook pasta according to package instructions. Drain.
3. In a pan, heat olive oil over medium heat. Warm marinara sauce.
4. Toss cooked pasta in the sauce, then layer with baked eggplant, mozzarella, and Parmesan.
5. Bake for 10-15 minutes until cheese is melted and bubbly.

Seafood Pasta

Ingredients:

- 8 oz spaghetti or linguine
- 1 lb mixed seafood (shrimp, mussels, calamari)
- 2 tablespoons olive oil
- 2 garlic cloves, minced
- 1/2 cup white wine
- 1/2 cup cherry tomatoes, halved
- 1/4 cup fresh parsley, chopped
- Salt and pepper to taste

Instructions:

1. Cook pasta according to package instructions. Drain, reserving some pasta water.
2. In a pan, heat olive oil over medium heat. Sauté garlic until fragrant, then add seafood. Cook until seafood is cooked through.
3. Add white wine and cherry tomatoes, simmer for 5 minutes.
4. Toss cooked pasta with the seafood mixture, adding reserved pasta water as needed. Season with salt, pepper, and parsley.
5. Serve immediately.

Ricotta and Spinach Cannelloni

Ingredients:

- 12 cannelloni shells
- 1 1/2 cups ricotta cheese
- 1 cup cooked spinach, chopped
- 1 egg
- 2 cups marinara sauce
- 1/4 cup grated Parmesan cheese
- Salt and pepper to taste

Instructions:

1. Preheat the oven to 375°F (190°C). Cook cannelloni shells according to package instructions. Drain and set aside.
2. In a bowl, combine ricotta, spinach, egg, salt, and pepper. Stuff the cannelloni shells with the mixture.
3. Place stuffed cannelloni in a baking dish and cover with marinara sauce. Sprinkle with Parmesan.
4. Bake for 25-30 minutes until bubbly and golden.

Pasta with Sun-Dried Tomato Pesto

Ingredients:

- 8 oz pasta (penne or spaghetti)
- 1/2 cup sun-dried tomatoes, chopped
- 1/4 cup pine nuts
- 1/4 cup Parmesan cheese
- 1/4 cup olive oil
- 1 garlic clove, minced
- Salt and pepper to taste

Instructions:

1. Cook pasta according to package instructions. Drain.
2. In a blender, combine sun-dried tomatoes, pine nuts, Parmesan, olive oil, garlic, salt, and pepper. Blend until smooth.
3. Toss cooked pasta in the pesto and serve immediately.

Pesto Lasagna

Ingredients:

- 9 lasagna noodles
- 2 cups ricotta cheese
- 2 cups mozzarella cheese, shredded
- 1 cup pesto sauce
- 1/2 cup grated Parmesan cheese
- 1/2 cup marinara sauce

Instructions:

1. Preheat the oven to 375°F (190°C). Cook lasagna noodles according to package instructions. Drain.
2. In a bowl, mix ricotta, mozzarella, Parmesan, and pesto sauce.
3. Layer cooked noodles with cheese mixture, marinara sauce, and pesto.
4. Bake for 30 minutes, then broil for 5 minutes until golden and bubbly.

Fusilli with Sausage and Broccoli Rabe

Ingredients:

- 8 oz fusilli pasta
- 1 lb Italian sausage, casings removed
- 1 bunch broccoli rabe, chopped
- 2 tablespoons olive oil
- 2 garlic cloves, minced
- 1/4 cup grated Parmesan cheese
- Salt and pepper to taste

Instructions:

1. Cook fusilli according to package instructions. Drain.
2. In a pan, cook sausage over medium heat until browned. Remove and set aside.
3. In the same pan, sauté garlic in olive oil. Add broccoli rabe and cook until tender.
4. Toss cooked fusilli, sausage, and broccoli rabe. Sprinkle with Parmesan and serve immediately.

Gnocchi with Tomato Basil Sauce

Ingredients:

- 1 lb gnocchi
- 2 cups marinara sauce
- 1 tablespoon olive oil
- 2 garlic cloves, minced
- 1/2 teaspoon dried basil
- 1/4 cup fresh basil, chopped
- 1/4 cup grated Parmesan cheese
- Salt and pepper to taste

Instructions:

1. Cook gnocchi according to package instructions. Drain.
2. In a pan, heat olive oil over medium heat. Sauté garlic until fragrant.
3. Add marinara sauce, dried basil, salt, and pepper. Simmer for 5 minutes.
4. Toss cooked gnocchi in the tomato basil sauce and top with fresh basil and Parmesan cheese.
5. Serve immediately.

Tortellini with Pesto and Peas

Ingredients:

- 1 package cheese tortellini
- 1 cup peas (fresh or frozen)
- 1/4 cup pesto sauce
- 2 tablespoons olive oil
- 1/4 cup grated Parmesan cheese
- Salt and pepper to taste

Instructions:

1. Cook tortellini according to package instructions. In the last 2 minutes of cooking, add peas to the boiling water.
2. Drain tortellini and peas, then toss them with pesto sauce and olive oil.
3. Season with salt and pepper, and sprinkle with Parmesan.
4. Serve immediately.

Pasta Carbonara with Peas

Ingredients:

- 8 oz spaghetti
- 4 oz pancetta or bacon, diced
- 2 eggs
- 1/2 cup grated Parmesan cheese
- 1 cup frozen peas, thawed
- 2 garlic cloves, minced
- Salt and pepper to taste

Instructions:

1. Cook spaghetti according to package instructions. Drain, reserving some pasta water.
2. In a pan, cook pancetta or bacon until crispy. Add garlic and sauté for 1 minute.
3. In a bowl, whisk eggs and Parmesan cheese.
4. Toss cooked pasta with pancetta and peas. Pour egg mixture over and stir quickly, adding reserved pasta water as needed to create a creamy sauce.
5. Serve immediately with extra Parmesan.

Spaghetti alla Caprese

Ingredients:

- 8 oz spaghetti
- 1 cup cherry tomatoes, halved
- 1/4 cup fresh mozzarella, cubed
- 2 tablespoons olive oil
- 1 tablespoon balsamic vinegar
- Fresh basil leaves, torn
- Salt and pepper to taste

Instructions:

1. Cook spaghetti according to package instructions. Drain.
2. In a bowl, combine cherry tomatoes, mozzarella, olive oil, balsamic vinegar, salt, and pepper.
3. Toss cooked spaghetti with the tomato mixture and fresh basil.
4. Serve immediately.

Roasted Garlic Pasta with Mushrooms

Ingredients:

- 8 oz pasta (linguine or spaghetti)
- 1 bulb garlic, roasted and mashed
- 1 cup mushrooms, sliced
- 2 tablespoons olive oil
- 1/2 cup heavy cream
- 1/4 cup grated Parmesan cheese
- Salt and pepper to taste

Instructions:

1. Roast garlic by placing the bulb in foil and baking at 400°F (200°C) for 25-30 minutes. Squeeze out the roasted garlic cloves.
2. Cook pasta according to package instructions. Drain.
3. In a pan, heat olive oil over medium heat and sauté mushrooms until tender.
4. Stir in roasted garlic, heavy cream, and Parmesan cheese. Simmer for 2 minutes.
5. Toss cooked pasta with the sauce and season with salt and pepper. Serve immediately.

Pesto Mac and Cheese

Ingredients:

- 8 oz elbow macaroni
- 1/2 cup pesto sauce
- 1 1/2 cups shredded cheddar cheese
- 1/2 cup milk
- 1 tablespoon butter
- Salt and pepper to taste

Instructions:

1. Cook macaroni according to package instructions. Drain.
2. In a pan, melt butter over medium heat and stir in milk and pesto sauce.
3. Add shredded cheddar cheese and cook until melted and smooth.
4. Toss cooked macaroni in the sauce. Season with salt and pepper.
5. Serve immediately.

Pasta with Spicy Sausage and Kale

Ingredients:

- 8 oz pasta (penne or rigatoni)
- 1 lb spicy Italian sausage, casings removed
- 2 cups kale, chopped
- 1/2 onion, chopped
- 2 garlic cloves, minced
- 1/4 cup white wine (optional)
- 1/2 cup grated Parmesan cheese
- Salt and pepper to taste

Instructions:

1. Cook pasta according to package instructions. Drain.
2. In a pan, cook sausage over medium heat until browned. Remove and set aside.
3. In the same pan, sauté onion and garlic until soft. Add kale and cook until wilted.
4. Deglaze the pan with white wine (if using) and cook for 1-2 minutes.
5. Toss cooked pasta with the sausage mixture and top with Parmesan cheese. Serve immediately.

Spaghetti with Lemon and Parmesan

Ingredients:

- 8 oz spaghetti
- 2 tablespoons olive oil
- 1/4 cup freshly squeezed lemon juice
- 1/2 cup grated Parmesan cheese
- Salt and pepper to taste
- Fresh parsley, chopped (optional)

Instructions:

1. Cook spaghetti according to package instructions. Drain.
2. In a pan, heat olive oil over medium heat. Add lemon juice, Parmesan, salt, and pepper.
3. Toss cooked spaghetti in the lemon and Parmesan sauce.
4. Garnish with fresh parsley and serve immediately.

Vegan Alfredo Pasta

Ingredients:

- 8 oz fettuccine or pasta of choice
- 1 cup raw cashews, soaked for 4 hours or overnight
- 1 cup water
- 2 tablespoons nutritional yeast
- 2 tablespoons lemon juice
- 1 garlic clove
- Salt and pepper to taste
- Fresh parsley, chopped for garnish

Instructions:

1. Cook pasta according to package instructions. Drain.
2. In a blender, combine soaked cashews, water, nutritional yeast, lemon juice, garlic, salt, and pepper. Blend until smooth.
3. Toss cooked pasta with the cashew Alfredo sauce.
4. Garnish with fresh parsley and serve immediately.